52 Weeks Of Gospel Magic
By Dennis Regling

COPYRIGHT 2008 Piedmont Christian Ministries
P O Box 118 Piedmont, Ohio 43983

www.magicministry.com

All scripture is from the King James Bible

This is dedicated to my loving wife, Karen.
Thank you for your continued support.

" *I thank my God upon every remembrance of you.*"
Philippians 1:3

The author
Dennis Regling

52 Weeks Of Gospel Magic

Introduction

Here are 52 magic tricks, or illusions, you can use to demonstrate Bible truths.

Without good patter, a trick is just a puzzle. With a good story line, the trick becomes a memorable illustration. I encourage you to develop your own unique presentations.

There is a memory verse at the beginning of each lesson.

3 Rules To Performing Magic

- Practice, practice, practice, and when you practice the moves, practice the patter. Make it uniquely yours. Most of the tricks have various applications, and I am sure you will come up with many.
- Never reveal how a trick is done. When the secret is revealed, the magic is gone. Don't ruin the audience's fun by revealing a trick, even if they beg you.
- Never do the same trick twice for the same audience. They will see the secret the second time. It is rare when you can fool them with the same illusion twice.

Gospel magic is a wonderful teaching tool, an interesting hobby and always new. Be sure to visit your local library and look up some magic books. They will have several. You can learn new tricks and how to build inexpensive props. With a little imagination, you can turn most tricks into a Bible lesson for your Sunday School class.

THE VALUE OF VISUAL AIDS

Visual aids have been regarded as great teaching aids since the beginning of time. God used them (The Potter, The Rainbow, The Burning Bush), Jesus used them (The Fig Tree, The Coin, The Loaves and Fishes), and every great communicator or teacher has used visual aids down through the ages.

Traditionally we think of visual aids used in church work as pictures, flannel graphs, maps and charts, props, puppets and more recently, video tapes. But sleight-of-hand tricks can also be effective visual aids for use in teaching the principles of Christianity.

Not only do sleight-of-hand tricks gain attention of audiences of all ages, but because of the mystery of not knowing how they are done, we tend to remember the trick longer. As a result this causes us to remember the lesson longer as well.

Too often, as beginners in magic all we concentrate on is learning new tricks. Don't make the same mistake others have made by ignoring the showmanship principles of this art form. Instead, take a professional attitude and learn how to make your effects more entertaining as well as more memorable.

The main difference between gospel magic and magic used in secular programs is that the aim of the gospel magician is not just to entertain, but to communicate Biblical truths.

The only purpose of the magic trick is to help you better illustrate the message. Never let the trick become more important than the message.

We remember so much longer the things we see, as oppose to the things we hear. For this reason it is most important that the things you teach with your tricks be the truth. Research the scriptures to be sure that the things you teach are Biblical.

Most importantly, always rely on the power of prayer before each presentation.

SHOULD CHRISTIANS PERFORM MAGIC?

Witchcraft and Sorcery are clearly condemned in the Word of God, but many Christians also lump the art of illusion and sleight of hand into this area as well.

Magicians for centuries have had a fascination with using little gremlins and demons in their advertising. Some will also appear to hypnotize their assistant to add to the mystery of the effect. The truth is, stage magicians never put anyone into a trance, it's just showmanship.

Several magicians go so far as to promote the lie that they possess special powers that enable them to accomplish the things they do. They may be possessed, but it is not with special powers.

This deception is only used by a few magicians, but is more widely used by so called mentalists, psychics, mediums, psychic surgeons, and saddest of all, so-called "Christian" Faith Healers. In Churches where honesty is taken for granted it is very easy for those so-called faith healers to deceive even the most intelligent. The art of illusion is designed for entertainment, not deception.

The practices of those above put a bad mark on the art, causing many to believe our art is satanic.

When people encounter things they do not understand, they often draw their own conclusions to help them justify the unexplainable. Unexplainable, due only to their lack of knowledge of the subject. Many Christians credit Satan with being in control of the things they don't understand.

Much of the misunderstanding is purely semantic. The Greek language, the original language of the Bible, is a very exact language. The Greek language uses two words in the Bible that have been translated into the word magic or magician.
The first is *pharmakos*, the second is *magos*.

Pharmakos, has three root meanings. The first meaning is "*the use of drugs*." It is from here that we get the words Pharmacist or Pharmacy. The second meaning is *the abuse of drugs*, and the third meaning is "*the abuse of drugs with the intent of harming another person*." This is Sorcery or Witchcraft and is clearly condemned in the Bible. In **Rev 21:8**, the original Greek uses the word *pharmakos,* which means Sorcerer. A sorcerer is one who uses drugs, potions, spells and enchantments.

The other Greek word, *magos,* means wise one, learned one or clever one. The word *Magos* is used in the Bible in reference to those who visited Jesus just after his birth as recorded in **Matthew 2:1**.

In **Daniel 5:11** this same word is used in reference to Daniel when he was made "*Master of the Magicians"*. This Godly young man was not being asked to head up the "sorcerers", which is a position I doubt he would have been interested in, but instead he was being asked to be the head of the king's "Learned" Council, or Cabinet.

Stage magicians use their art (and it is a learned art, like singing or playing a musical instrument), to entertain and make people laugh. That, according to scripture is Biblical. "*A merry heart doeth good like a medicine: but a broken spirit drieth the bones.*"

Proverbs 17:22.
Sleight-of-hand illusions can also be used as a teaching aid. We learn a lot more by what we see then we do by what we hear. We retain 5 times as much information that comes through our eyes as as we do that which comes through our ears.

I make it very clear in my programs that what I am doing is strictly sleight of hand, optical illusions and object lessons to more clearly illustrate Christian principals. There are no "paranormal powers," and no occult activity.

A tent full of folks watching the author present magical illusions. Everyone loves "magic." More importantly, everyone needs to hear the Gospel of Jesus Christ.

This page left blank on purpose.

WARNING:

Some of the following effects use matches and/or household chemicals.

Children should not perform these effects without adult supervision.

Week 1

Romans 6:23 *For the wages of sin is death; but the gift of God is eternal life through Jesus Christ our Lord*

Dealing With Sin

A VERY Powerful Object lesson using chemicals. You will be amazed at the chemical reaction the first time you do this routine.

Items needed for message:
- 2 - large jars - Large mouth top / with lids
- You need to be able to freely fit your hand inside
- 1- White cotton handkerchief
- Heavy duty spray starch
- 1- bottle iodine -(red) - helps to have skull and crossbones on front of bottle this will add to presentation
- Sodium Sulfite (Photo grade) - You can purchase this at any photo shop. It is used in developing film.

Preparation:
1. Mark one of the jar lids WORKS
2. Mark the other jar lid FORGIVENESS
3. Prior to presentation 1 hour approx. Spray entire open handkerchief with starch, both sides,. heavy application. Then allow handkerchief to hang and air dry.
4. After handkerchief dries, fold handkerchief into halves 3 times. (making a small square)
5. A few minutes before presentation - fill both jars 1/2 full of Warm water. (the water must be very warm for chemicals to work properly.)

6   Place 4 heaping tablespoons of Sodium Sulfite into jar marked WORKS

7   Spray starch approx. 3 seconds into jar marked WORKS

8   Place both jars a few feet apart on the presentation table with chemicals etc. out of sight. Folded starched handkerchief should be placed on table out of view of audience, yet within your reach.

The Presentation

Who can tell me what sin is?
Right, sin is when we do what we know we shouldn't do.

The Bible says, "**Romans 6:23** *For the wages of sin is death; but the gift of God is eternal life through Jesus Christ our Lord.*"

(Show the bottle of Iodine)

See the skull and crossbones on the bottle. This means it is poison. If we were to drink this we would die. It is a symbol of death.

Well that's what the Bible tells us about sin. In other words, if your sins are not forgiven, you earn death. That is, you will go to hell rather than living forever with Jesus.

(Take lid off iodine)

Consider this hankey. It is clean, but if we add some sin, it becomes stained.

Place the handkerchief over the Iodine bottle and turn upside down to allow Iodine to soak through several layers of the handkerchief. Do this five times once in each corner of the handkerchief and once in the middle.

When we sin by disobeying God, it stains our lives. (Open handkerchief up to show it entirely.)

You may think, "Hey it's no problem. All I have to do is be good and do good deeds. Then I can get to Heaven"

Take handkerchief and dunk several times into jar ladled WORKS. The water will turn a Very murky dark purple color. The handkerchief will lose all the spots but turn to a dark purple color.

There is a scripture in the BIBLE that tells us our works are as filthy rags. Even if we try hard to be a good person, those things won't get us to Heaven. Our sin is a huge stain that fills our lives.

Only Jesus Christ can forgive our sins and wash us as white as snow. When Jesus died on the cross, he took our sins with him. He suffered death for us. If we believe on the Lord Jesus Christ we can be saved.

(Dip the stained handkerchief into the jar marked FORGIVENESS - dip several times. As you do this the stains will come off and the water will remain clear.)

Show handkerchief clean and washed.

Jesus came to earth so that he could be our sacrifice for all the sins we have committed or ever will commit. All we have to do is believe on him. To believe that he is God's ONLY begotten son and that anyone who believes in him will not perish but will live forever with him in Heaven.

(Dip handkerchief several times back into the jar marked WORKS - the murky purple water will become clear again.)

When we tell others about JESUS they too can know the way to be forgiven and free from sin. They too will get to spend eternal life with JESUS in heaven.

Week 2

1 John 5:13 *These things have I written unto you that believe on the name of the Son of God; that ye may know that ye have eternal life, and that ye may believe on the name of the Son of God.*

Salvation Is Not a Gamble

This is a great routine for any type of utility device, such as a change bag, a dove pan, or an Indian Sweet Vase. You can also make a simple utility switch bag.

Take two 9x12 or similar size manila mailing envelopes. Cut one of them along all the folds. This will leave you a 9x12 piece that when slipped into the other envelope will give you a perfect divider.

Start with an extra envelope with some silliness written on it in the side of the divider where the clasp is. During the routine, you will put the first two envelopes on the same side. You will place an envelope with a $5 on the other side of the divider.

If you fold down the flap on the envelope over the divider, the divider will be hidden. Your volunteers will only see the 3 envelopes on the front side. After they take their choices, you can casually open the flap out. Do this as you look in as if you cannot find the little envelope. Remove the envelope with the bill and place your switch envelope aside.

Effect:
Three envelopes are loaded - two with useless information, and one with a $5 bill. They are all placed into a bag, mixed up, and two spectators are given a free choice of which envelope they want. If they get the $5 bill, it's theirs to keep. The magician keeps the envelope not chosen. After making their choices, it is revealed that the spectators chose the useless papers, and the magician ends up with the $5 bill every time.

Setup:
One of the envelopes, with a useless message, is loaded into one side of the utility prop. The audience is unaware of the presence of this envelope.

Presentation:
Select 2 spectators to come and help you, and in their presence, load all 3 remaining envelopes with one item each. Two will hold useless papers with silly messages, and the third will have the $5 bill. Place the envelopes, one at a time, into the bag (or utility device), making sure that the first two (holding useless papers) go into the same side as the hidden 4th envelope. The envelope with the $5 bill is placed in last, in the section opposite the other envelopes.

Now shake the bag, and offer each of the spectators a "free" choice of any of the three envelopes. What they take is what they get, and you will keep whatever is left over. Allow them to take any of the useless envelopes, and once they have made their choices, you reach in and take out the envelope holding the $5 bill.

Gospel Presentation:

"How can we know for sure that Jesus is the only way for man to get to heaven? What if eternal life were just a game of chance? And if it were, what would the odds be? Let's run a little "experiment", shall we?

"Here are 3 envelopes, each one identical to the others. We'll load each of the them with something, only two of the "somethings" will be worth "nothing". The third envelope will be loaded with a $5 bill, and for the purposes of this illustration, the $5 will represent heaven. The goal of this experiment is to pick the envelope with the $5 bill!

"I'll pick two helpers, and we'll place all three envelopes into this bag. Let's shake them up so no one knows which one is which, and then each of you may select any envelope you want. Just remember, whichever one you take is what you get and I will get to keep whatever one is left behind, okay?"

(Spectators select their envelopes, and magician gets the one with the $5 bill)

Have each volunteer open their envelope and read the slip of paper. You can put funny sayings on each.

Open your envelope and reveal the $5 bill.

Isn't it great that God doesn't make our eternal reward just a game of chance? **1 John 5:13** says, *"These things have I written unto you that believe on the name of the Son of God; that ye may know that ye have eternal life, and that ye may believe on the name of the Son of God."*

"That's our confidence!! We can KNOW where we are going! It's not a gamble it's a promise!"

It's good if you have a small prize for each of your volunteers. A bookmark or candy bar are great choices.

Don't gamble on your future. Believe on the Lord Jesus Christ.

Week 3

Romans 3:23 *For all have sinned, and come short of the glory of God;*

Which Way?

Effect: An arrow that is clearly pointing one way is seen to instantly, and visibly change direction.

Materials Needed: A sign depicting HEAVEN, a sign depicting HELL, a picture of a large arrow, a clear water glass, pitcher of water. Note: The glass should be made of glass, and not plastic. It may still work with plastic, but we're looking for the smoothest, clearest finish, as we will be looking through the glass to see the arrow.

Presentation: As Christians, we believe that there is an ultimate goal, or direction for our lives. It is an eternity spent in Heaven, with our Lord. However, as you will see by looking at our display, there is a built-in problem with our being able to reach that goal. You see, we all have sin in our lives (Rom 3:23), and that sin prevents us from heading in a direction toward Heaven, and actually steers us toward Hell!

Today, we are going to perform a demonstration of what happens to a person's life, the moment he or she believes on Jesus to be their Lord.

I'll place this clear glass (or jar) in front of the arrow, and you can still clearly see that the arrow points toward the sign marked HELL.

Our lives are to be as vessels, willing and able to hold whatever we put into them. Looking at our example, it would appear that no matter how "clean and clear" our lives appear to be, without the Lord Jesus, we are not only empty inside, but we are headed for an eternity in Hell, apart from Christ.

Let's suggest, just for a moment, however, that the water in this glass (hold up glass of water) represents the Word of God. We know from **John 1:1** *"In the beginning was the Word, and the Word was with God, and the Word was God."*

In other words, when we refer to the Word, we are also referencing Jesus Christ Himself.

And let's take a look at what happens when we allow the Word, (or Jesus) to come into our lives by asking Him to forgive our sins, and change our eternal destination. (Pour the glass of water into the first glass (jar), and watch as before your very eyes, the direction of the arrow appears to change, to point toward HEAVEN!

Look at that!! What this little illusion is showing us is a truth that can change our very lives for an eternity! If we would only ask the Lord to forgive us of our sins, He is faithful and just to do just that! And the change in our eternal destination is an instant thing! When Christ is in us, and we are in Him, we are on our way to Heaven. and that is a truth worth shouting about!

Additional Note: This little illusion is an illusion for the eyes, but it is also a scientific principle in action - that of "refraction". Refraction is what happens when light is "bent" through a lens of some sort, and just such a lens is created when we add the water to the clear glass. Have fun with this. Not only can you show the audience a nifty little science lesson, but you can share the truth that is capable of changing their lives for an eternity!

It's not how we think we look, it's how God says we are that matters. Remember to use the looking glass of God's Word.

Week 4

John 3:16 *For God so loved the world, that he gave his only begotten Son, that whosoever believeth in him should not perish, but have everlasting life.*

Effect: Despite a completely free choice, and a genuine shuffle of 2 packs of cards, the spectator and performer discover that they BOTH selected the SAME card, at the SAME time!

Materials Needed: You need 2 identical packs of cards. These may be playing cards, picture cards, or alphabet cards. The only criteria is that all of the cards be unique, with **no duplicates**. I prefer Uno cards as some church folks object to regular playing cards.

Presentation: Allow your spectator to choose between two identical packs of cards. You will take the pack left behind. Instruct your spectator to copy each move you make, in the following order:
- Shuffle the pack. Exchange packs.
- Shuffle the pack again. Exchange packs again.
- Choose any card, look at it and remember it, and put it on the top of the pack.
- Cut the pack, losing your selected card in the middle somewhere.
- Exchange packs again.
- Look through the pack, and remove the chosen card, face down.
- Have the spectator turn over his card, and then turn over yours which is the "perfect match" to his!

The Secret: After you shuffle your spectator's pack in step 3, peek at what card is on the bottom of his pack before handing it back to him in step 4. In this way, you will immediately be able to find his card after step 6, because his card will be the one immediately on TOP of the card you peeked, (when the cards are FACING YOU!).

It is important that you pull out HIS card, and not the one you "looked at" during step 5. Add a little drama, and you have an award winning illusion on your hands!

Gospel Application: Ever wonder about all those shows on late night television that suggest that someone can just pick up the phone, and dial 1-800-GO-PSYCHO... I mean psychic, and the person on the other end of the line will tell you all about what you've done, and are going to do? Boy, those commercials sure look like those people have real PSYCHO, I mean psychic abilities, don't they?

Let's ask a question;. is it possible to know the future? Is it possible for a mere human being to know something before it ever happens? For real?

Before you answer that, let's run a test.

Here on the table, I have two packets of cards. Let's run a completely unique test using these two packs of cards, and someone from the audience.

At this time, go through the routine, exactly as detailed above. Immediately following the revelation that your cards match, come back to this line of discussion.

Proof of psychic ability? Absolutely NOT! What you just saw **was not** a coincidence, but a well-thought out, and perfectly executed plan. It was just an illusion and yet, let's go back to the original question.

Is it possible for mere man to KNOW what will happen before it ever occurs? My friends, the answer is yes!

Now, don't get angry with me. Let me explain.
According to **John 3:16**, I can confidently say that I KNOW that I am going to Heaven! I have that assurance, because I have received Christ as my Lord.

Can I know YOUR future? Absolutely not! In fact, it is an abomination to the Lord even to mess with such things as divination, or any other type of witchcraft or astrology. But YOU can know YOUR eternal future. You can know for sure that you are saved by the blood of Jesus. Do you have that assurance?

Week 5
Mobius Madness

1 John 5:11 *And this is the record, that God hath given to us eternal life, and this life is in his Son.*

A Mobius strip doesn't have 2 sides - but in fact, has only 1 side, which is both the inside and the outside, or if you prefer, the top and the bottom at the same time!

And the best part is: <u>YOU can MAKE one</u> for yourself! And more to the point - you can create an actual illusion with your mobius strip.

How to make a Mobius strip:
1. Cut or tear a strip of newspaper, about 2" thick, down the entire length of page (top to bottom).
2. Half-twist one end (180°), and glue (or tape) it to the other end, forming a loop. (Make some with no twists, and some with a full twist (360°) to turn this into a great trick!)

Making it a Trick:
Now that you have made your Mobius strip, you can show the audience that it really does only have one side, by tracing your finger all along the path. But with the strip in this condition, there's even more that you can do!

If you cut a loop that has not been twisted, right down the center of the loop, it does just what you expect it to do. It makes two loops the same size!

If, however, you cut your Mobius strip in the same way, you will be amazed to discover that it does not make two loops, but instead, it makes one loop, twice the size of the original!

And, if you cut the strip that you made with a full twist, you will discover that it makes two loops, BUT the two loops that it makes, are linked, one inside the other! This is a real fooler!

Note: *In order for this to appear "magical", you must not allow the audience to know that you have changed any of the loops. The assumption should be that all the loops are the same, which greatly enhances the effect.*

Presentation:
(Pick up the non-gimmicked loop) I love circles! They are so cool! They have no beginning, and no end, and that reminds me of God! The word that describes that is, "eternal". Eternal means, "without beginning or end, everlasting".

The Bible tells us of a time, when God sent His Son, Jesus, into the world. And even though Jesus was born as a human, he never gave up his deity, which means, He still had the nature of God! (cut the ungimmicked loop, to show 2 separate, but identical loops).

(Pick up the loop that was twisted with a FULL twist). The Bible tells us that God created us in His image and likeness. That doesn't mean we are "eternal", because in fact, the very fact that we are created means that we had a beginning. But there is something about us, that is just like something about God, as shown by this loop, that looks remarkably similar to the first loop I showed you. You know, God sent Jesus, so that we might ask Him into our hearts, and be eternally together with God! (Cut the loop, and show that now there are 2 loops linked).

(Pick up the loop that was twisted with a half twist). God must have a lot of love for us to send His only Son, don't you think? How much love would that take? I don't know, but it probably is BIGGER than we can imagine! (tear the loop, and show that it has grown to double the size).

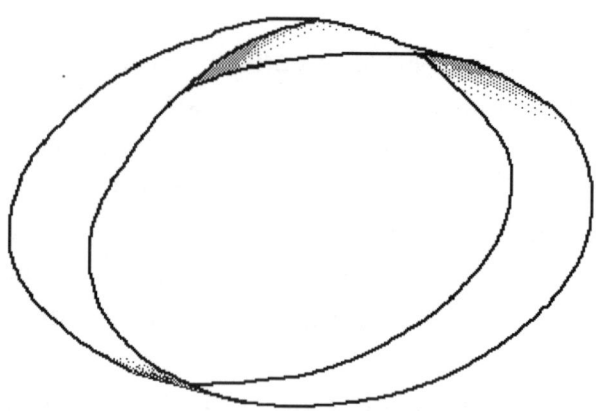

Week 6

The Classified Prediction

Revelation 3:8 *I know thy works: behold, I have set before thee an open door, and no man can shut it: for thou hast a little strength, and hast kept my word, and hast not denied my name.*

Presentation: I use this to demonstrate how God knows every little detail of our lives. A want ad often details a need of the advertiser. God knows our needs even before we ask!

Effect: The magician shows a column from the classified advertisements out of a newspaper to the audience. He announces that he is going to cut the strip in half, and that he will let someone else tell him exactly where to cut it. The magician tells them to say "STOP" while he moves the scissors up and down. He gives them a chance to change their mind and cuts it where he is told. He tells them to read the first line of the newspaper strip, and a sealed envelope is picked up off the table and is an exact prediction, word for word.

Secret: Cut a long strip out of the classifieds and cut the first article or so off of the top. On a piece of paper, write down the first line or two of the article on the long strip. Fold the piece of paper and seal it in the envelope. Before beginning the trick, lay the envelope down somewhere discretely. Hold the strip *upside down* and you can cut it anywhere because the predicted line is on the bottom.

Week 7

Linking Ropes

Mark 9:23 *Jesus said unto him, If thou canst believe, all things are possible to him that believeth.*

Effect: Show three pieces of rope. The ends have been marked with colored tape so you can tell them apart. One rope is marked with red tape, one with blue, and one with yellow. The ropes are tied into three separate rings. The three rings are tossed in the air and Presto -- they join together and form one huge ring of rope! The giant ring may be tossed for examination -- they'll find nothing!! This is great visual magic.

The Secret: This is a simple, yet dazzling effect. What you need is some soft rope (cotton clothesline with the core removed works great) and three different colors of vinyl tape. Cut three pieces of rope, approximately 16" long. Cut 2 pieces of each color tape, about 1" long each.

For example's sake, we will assume you have red, blue and yellow. Wrap the tapes around the ends of the rope - but - make the ends different colors. One rope will have a red and a blue end, another a red and a yellow end and the third a blue and a yellow end. When performing, grasp the ropes in your hand so that they extend out both sides of your hand. Be sure that on each side there is a red, yellow and blue end. This creates the illusion that one rope has 2 blue ends, one has 2 red ends, etc.

Now, take the 2 red ends and tie them into a loop, always retaining the middles of the ropes under your fingers. Do the same with the blue and the yellow ends. It will now appear that you have 3 small loops in your hand.

Presentation:
Folks are always saying that one thing or another is impossible. Today you can fly all over the world in airplanes, yet not too long ago, folks thought it was impossible for man to fly.

You might look at these three little loops of rope and think it is impossible for me to pass them over my feet, up my body and over my head. Yet, it is not.

With a bit of showmanship, toss the loops in the air, or quickly expand them in your hands to show that 3 small loops have "magically" become one large loop. Step through them.

When I examine my own life and my past, I know it is impossible for me to earn eternal life. When Adam and Eve sinned, it looked impossible that man would ever again have fellowship with God.

But God does the impossible and he raised Jesus from the dead that we might have eternal life by believing in him.

Notes: This is an impressive and surprising illusion. Perhaps the 3 loops will represent how we act at home, in school and with our friends, and the big loop demonstrates how we should have integrity, being the same person, treating folks the same all the time.
The three loops can also represent God the Father, Son and Holy Ghost and how they are separate yet one.

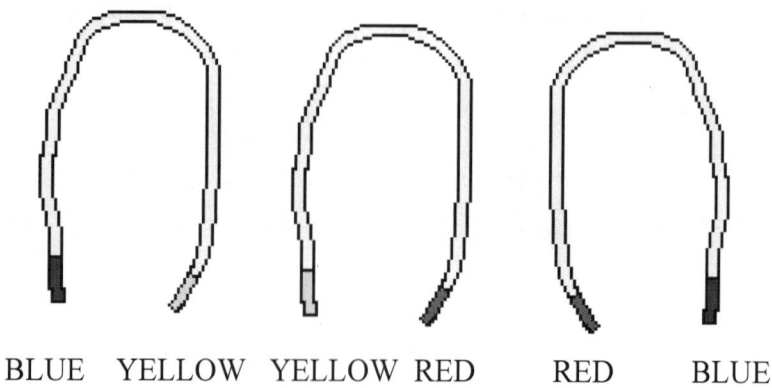

BLUE　　YELLOW　　YELLOW　　RED　　　RED　　　BLUE

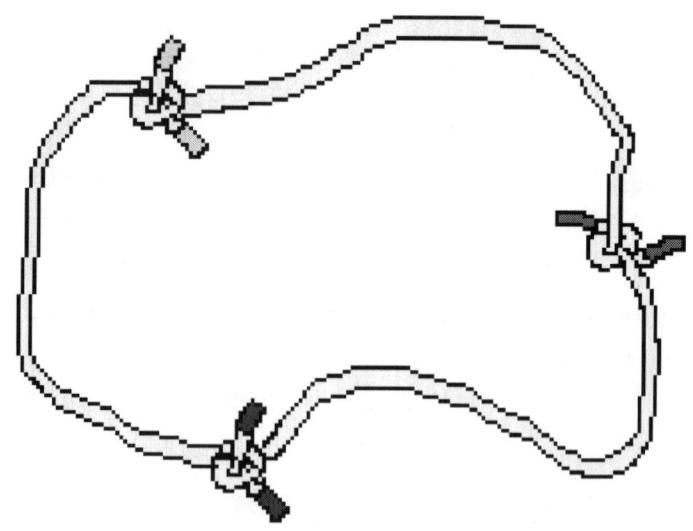

Week 8

Card In Wallet Prediction: The promises of God, and his knowledge of the hidden things.

Isaiah 45:3 *And I will give thee the treasures of darkness, and hidden riches of secret places, that thou mayest know that I, the LORD, which call thee by thy name, am the God of Israel.*

Effect: The magician lets a spectator pick a card. Then, the magician takes a card out of his or her wallet and it matches the card chosen by the spectator! Again, you can use Uno cards or picture cards.

Secret:
- First, you need two of the same card (they don't need to be from the same type of deck). Let's say it is the queen of diamonds.
- Take one of the queens and put it in a wallet. Put either double stick tape or a loop of tape on the bottom of the wallet, and put the wallet in your pocket. (An envelope may be used instead of a wallet.)
- Take the other queen and put it on top of the deck you want to use.
- Now you are ready to do the trick.
- Take out the wallet and tell the spectator that there is a prediction of some sort inside (make sure the spectator does not see the tape).
- Tell a spectator to pick a card and **not** to look at it.

- Take the card and put it on top of the deck.
- Now, start to talk about ESP and casually put the wallet over the deck of cards. When the wallet is removed, the card the spectator selected is on the bottom of the wallet, and the queen of diamonds is now on the top of the deck.
- Put the queen of diamonds on the table and flip it over.
- Slowly open the wallet to build up the suspense and finally reveal the card matches. That person just may look at you differently the next time you see him or her.

Week 9

Peter Escapes. The Lord delivers us in the time of trials. He will never forsake us.

Acts 12:6-11 *And when Herod would have brought him forth, the same night Peter was sleeping between two soldiers, bound with two chains: and the keepers before the door kept the prison. And, behold, the angel of the Lord came upon him, and a light shined in the prison: and he smote Peter on the side, and raised him up, saying, Arise up quickly. And his chains fell off from his hands. And the angel said unto him, Gird thyself, and bind on thy sandals. And so he did. And he saith unto him, Cast thy garment about thee, and follow me. And he went out, and followed him; and wist not that it was true which was done by the angel; but thought he saw a vision. When they were past the first and the second ward, they came unto the iron gate that leadeth unto the city; which opened to them of his own accord: and they went out, and passed on through one street; and forthwith the angel departed from him. And when Peter was come to himself, he said, Now I know of a surety, that the Lord hath sent his angel, and hath delivered me out of the hand of Herod, and from all the expectation of the people of the Jews.*

This is a simple trick, but presented well, it is a great visual to the story. As with all the illusions in this book, the message is what is most important.

Effect: The magician lets the spectator pick a card. This card represents Peter in jail. Then the deck is shuffled by the spectator. After that, the magician says the card will be reversed in the deck, the jailers know where Peter is. He is under their command. Really, he is not. The magician then pulls the card out of his pocket.

Procedure:
- Before you start the trick you need to get two cards that are identical.
- Put one of the two identical cards in your pocket and the other on the top of the deck.
- You can now start the trick.
- Divide the deck into four piles keeping in mind which pile the top card is in.
- Ask the spectator to pick two piles. If one of the chosen piles has the identical card on top, put the piles that were not chosen to the side. If both of the chosen piles do not have the identical card on top, put the chosen piles to the side.
- One of the two remaining piles should now have the identical card on top. Have the spectator choose a pile and discard one of the piles by the same manner as before.
- Give the spectator the top card and put the deck back together. Have the spectator put the card back in the deck and shuffle it. Say the card is reversed in the deck, and when it is not found to be reversed, take the card out of your pocket and say, "sometimes it jumps too far."

Week 10

The Four Christians:

Jeremiah 23:3 *And I will gather the remnant of my flock out of all countries whither I have driven them, and will bring them again to their folds; and they shall be fruitful and increase.*

God will gather his people together from all nations. A message on evangelism.

Effect: The magician shows a spectator four aces that represent missionaries. The aces are placed in various locations in the deck. The magician then pulls the same four aces off the top!

Method:
- You need the four aces out of a deck of cards.
- Then put any three cards behind the aces and fan out the four aces so the spectator can't see the three cards in back
- Put the cards together and put them on top of the deck.
- Tell a story about four missionaries who go throughout the world. Take the top card (which should be one of the three random cards) and put it in near the bottom of the deck.
Say that missionary is going to Australia. (Down under - get it?)

- Put the next card from the top of the deck near the middle of the deck and say the missionary is going to the South Sea Islands.
- Put the next card near the top of the deck and say the missionary is going to Asia.
- Keep the next card on the top saying the missionary is going to Canada.
- When Jesus returns, he will gather his flock from throughout the world. Now take the top four cards of the top of the deck and they will be the aces.

Until Jesus returns, we need to be busy taking the Gospel to the entire world.

Week 11

Shipwrecked: Continuing in the faith.

Timothy 1:19 *Holding faith, and a good conscience; which some having put away concerning faith have made shipwreck:*

Effect: A deck is cut as many times as the spectator wants and then the cards are dealt out in perfect order.

Secret:
·First, you need to find all of the aces, kings, queens, and jacks and take them out of the deck.
·Arrange them in the order of ace, king, queen, then jack, ace, king, queen, then jack and so on.
·Tell a story about how the ship, which is the deck, crashes and is thrown forward. When you say this have the spectator cut the deck forward.
·Then tell how the ship tries to get out of the storm by weaving and that the storm just gets worse and worse and cut the deck as many times as the spectator wants.
·Deal the cards one at a time to the four corners of the table and tell how when the ship hit the big rock the four families went to four separate islands and that is just so happened that the families ended up on the same islands.
·Flip over the four stacks of cards and show that all aces, kings, queens, and jacks are separated by pile!

Message: We need to be found among like-minded Believers. **Hebrews 10:25**

Week 12
Smoke Signals

Philippians 4:6 *Be careful for nothing; but in every thing by prayer and supplication with thanksgiving let your requests be made known unto God.*

The American Indians sent messages via smoke signals. We communicate with God through our prayers. Our prayers ascend to heaven like the smoke from a fire.

Effect: The magician hands a spectator a piece of paper and tells him to write any number between 1 and 100 on the paper. The magician turns his back while the number is written and then turns back around and folds up the paper and rips it up. The magician proceeds to burn the paper and put his hand over the smoke for a few seconds and tells the spectator the correct number.

Secret:

- Before you start the trick you need a book of matches, a surface safe for burning, a 3" piece of paper, and an inner coat pocket.

- You are now ready to begin the trick.

- Show the spectator the paper and tell him or her to write any number between 1 and 100 and keep the writing small in order to be inconspicuous.

- While the number is being written, turn your back to show that you don't see them writing it.

- Turn back around and fold the paper into quarters. The number will be inside the corner opposite the open end.

·Tear the paper into quarters and keep the corner with the number on top of the stack closest to you.

·Keep that piece between your thumb and palm while you burn the rest of the paper.

·While the spectator is watching the burning paper, (because lets face it, nobody can resist watching fire) put the matches into your inner coat pocket with the hand that you have the number and take a quick glance at the number and put it as well in the pocket.

·Now you know the number in your head and have nothing to worry about. Put your hand over the smoke and say that you're picking up something.

Keep the suspense going as long as you can, then tell the correct number and let the spectator stare at you in amazement.

Week 13
Rising Ring (Ascension of Christ)

1 Thessalonians 4:17 *Then we which are alive and remain shall be caught up together with them in the clouds, to meet the Lord in the air: and so shall we ever be with the Lord.*

Needed: a rubber band, a finger ring

Presentation: Take a rubber band and break it. About half way up the rubber band grab the band between you left pointer finger and thumb. Place the ring against your fingers with the rubber band through it and place your right pointer finger and thumb on the other side of the band. Hold the right side up about 45 degrees and slowly let the rubber band out of your left hand. The ring will go up and the spectators won't see the excess band in your left hand.

Message: Jesus promised he would return for his church. On that day, we will be taken to be with him forever. How can we prepare to be ready for that day?

Week 14
Linking Clips (Two in Agreement)

Matthew 18:19 *Again I say unto you, That if two of you shall agree on earth as touching any thing that they shall ask, it shall be done for them of my Father which is in heaven.*

Needed: a dollar bill, two paperclips

Presentation: Fold a dollar bill in thirds. It should be the front of the bill, middle behind that then the other end behind that. Place a paper clip on the left two front flaps and place a paper clip on the left back two flaps. When you yank the dollar bill apart the paper clips will be linked inside each other.

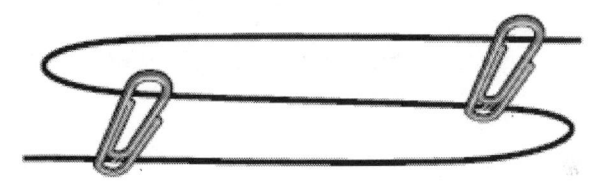

Message: Matthew 18:15-20 If a professed Christian is wronged by another, he ought not to complain of it to others, as is often done merely upon report, but to go to the offender privately, state the matter kindly, and show him his conduct. This would generally have all the desired effect with a true Christian, and the parties would be reconciled.

In all our proceedings we should seek direction in prayer; we cannot too highly prize the promises of God. Wherever and whenever we meet in the name of Christ, we should consider him as present in the midst of us.

Week 15

Light a used match (restoring your fire for the Lord)

Luke 15:32 *It was meet that we should make merry, and be glad: for this thy brother was dead, and is alive again; and was lost, and is found.*

The story of the prodigal son is a great one to share with youngsters. It can be used to show how God is ready to forgive us, no matter where we have traveled.

Effect: You take out a box of matches and go to light a candle but when you open them they are all used.

You then say I hate that when people put used matches back in the box. "Oh sorry it was me. I hate it when I do that."
Take out the used match and strike it and it lights.

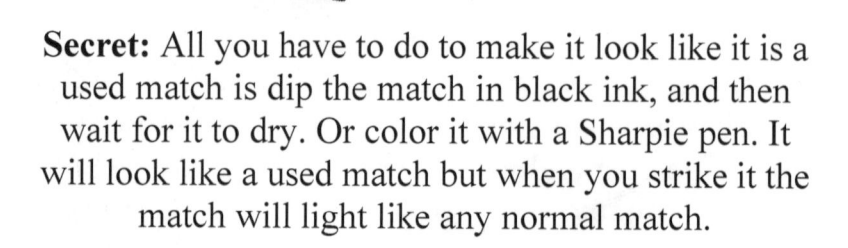

Secret: All you have to do to make it look like it is a used match is dip the match in black ink, and then wait for it to dry. Or color it with a Sharpie pen. It will look like a used match but when you strike it the match will light like any normal match.

Week 16

Changing Liquid

2 Corinthians 5:17 *Therefore if any man be in Christ, he is a new creature: old things are passed away; behold, all things are become new.*

Effect: The magician places a handkerchief over a glass of colored liquid and when he removes it the liquid has changed to water.

Message: The Bible is clear that when we become a Christian, our life changes from the inside. Now this liquid is anything but clear. But when I put the cloth over the glass, the glass and liquid are in the cloth. A person who is in Christ and has Christ in him changes and we see now that the liquid has also changed.

Secret: Cut a thin piece of colored plastic to fit the glass. Pour water up to the top of the plastic. This will give the illusion that the liquid is colored. When you place the handkerchief on the glass remove the plastic with the handkerchief leaving clear water.

Week 17.
Empty Matchbox (Loaves & Fishes)

Philippians 4:19 *But my God shall supply all your need according to his riches in glory by Christ Jesus.*

Effect: The magician shows an empty matchbox and when he close it it becomes full.

Luke 9:11-17 *And the people, when they knew it, followed him: and he received them, and spake unto them of the kingdom of God, and healed them that had need of healing. And when the day began to wear away, then came the twelve, and said unto him, Send the multitude away, that they may go into the towns and country round about, and lodge, and get victuals: for we are here in a desert place. But he said unto them, Give ye them to eat. And they said, We have no more but five loaves and two fishes; except we should go and buy meat for all this people. For they were about five thousand men. And he said to his disciples, Make them sit down by fifties in a company. And they did so, and made them all sit down. Then he took the five loaves and the two fishes, and looking up to heaven, he blessed them, and brake, and gave to the disciples to set before the multitude. And they did eat, and were all filled: and there was taken up of fragments that remained to them twelve baskets.*

Preparation: Lay a row of matches inside the matchbox cover supported by the edge of the matchbox. Start with the empty box open, the matches concealed above. When you close the box, the matches on the cover fall into the box. Or you can show two matches, one is loaves, one is fishes. Add them to the seemingly empty box then they multiply.

Week 18

Turning Cups (Follow The Lord)

John 10:27 *My sheep hear my voice, and I know them, and they follow me:*

Effect: Explain that you can turn three cups, two at a time and with three moves, have them end up all facing up. Then when spectator tries (doing exact same moves) they all end up face down! This can be repeated many times with the same outcome.

Living a Christian life can seem impossible without the Lord's direction. Even when we watch others around us, even those that are doing right, we may still find ourselves failing. That is why it is so important to read our Bible and listen to the Lord's voice.

Psalms 119:105 *Thy word is a lamp unto my feet, and a light unto my path.* Even with the lights on, we are in a spiritual blindness. We cannot see what we ought to do at times. Too often, we go on our own knowledge and feelings we often get the wrong results.

Let me demonstrate this to you. I am going to flip some cups, 2 at a time until all the cups are face up. I will do this in exactly 3 moves. If you watch me, you may think you can do it, too. We will see.

Then, when you fail, I will instruct you perfectly, as Christ instructs us in life. Then you will be able to go home and fool Mom and Dad.

Presentation: Start with three cups of glasses on a table in following position from left to right: face down, face up, face down. Now take the two cups on right side and flip them over. Then take the two outside cups and flip them. Finally flip the two cups on the right side. Of course they end up all facing up. Here's where the trick comes in. Take the middle cup and flip it over while telling a spectator that they're going to do the exact same thing you just did. The cups are now facing, from left to right: face up, down, up. This is different then you started but this won't be noticeable. Tell them to do exactly what you did before, and when they do, they will end up all face down.

"Mr. Dennis" before an assembly of school students.

Week 19.
Quick Mind Reading Trick

Acts 8:9 *But there was a certain man, called Simon, which beforetime in the same city used sorcery, and bewitched the people of Samaria, giving out that himself was some great one:*

Effect: Ask someone to think of a number between 1 and 50 and say wait before you do that , the 2 digits of the number you are thinking of must be both odd and different. You can't use 11, but you could choose 13. When you have a number raise your hand.

You then call out 37 and wait for the expression on their face. This works because because 7 out of 10 times they will pick this number.

This trick is so good, David Blaine did it on his first TV special.

If you want this to work every time, write the numbers 13,15,17,19,31,35,37 and 39 on eight slips of paper and have one in each of 8 pockets. Pull out the one a spectator names and it matches.

Another way to do this trick is to have everyone think of a number.

Instruct them that you will call out a number and if it matches theirs, they are to stand and clap.

When you call out 37, almost everyone in the room will be giving you a standing ovation.

In today's Bible verse, we see where Simon was tricking people into thinking he had magic powers. A lot of people today will try to convince you they are "great ones."

MTV wants to tell you how to dress, your teachers may try to tell you how to think, magazines may tell you what to buy but when these things don't line up with the Bible, you need to remember what God has said and not be fooled.

The best way not to let the devil fool you is by reading your Bible every day and memorizing God's word.

Simon wasn't as great as he put forth.
Read Acts chapter 8 to learn how God humbled him.

Week 20.

Magical Matches!

Proverbs 27:17 *Iron sharpeneth iron; so a man sharpeneth the countenance of his friend.*

Effect: a "charged up" match or toothpick touches another, and is sent flying about four feet up!

A "charged-up Christian" can encourage others.

Materials: 2 toothpicks or match sticks.

Presentation: Take the two sticks and let your audience examine them. Put one stick on your hand leaving 1/3 of the stick sticking out. Take the other stick with your hand and put it under the other stick. Without them noticing, flick the bottom of the stick in your hand with your middle finger. If done right, the stick in your hand should go "jump". Pretend to charge up a stick on your shirt. Then let them try.

Week 22

What To Do When You Feel Tempted
Balloon Magic Trick You Can Do

Effect: This is an easy version of the commercial magic trick. Blow up a party balloon and with a small pin, you puncture the balloon but it doesn't pop!

Method: Blow up a round party balloon. It should be about 12" in diameter. Tie it off. You also need a straight pin, a diaper pin, or a hat pin. I get extra laughs by using the diaper pin.

Take some clear tape (Scotch Brand, etc.) and on the side opposite the knot, place a small square of tape on the nipple or thick part of the balloon. You might also put a piece on the side of the balloon.

Holding the balloon in one hand and the pin in the other push the pin into the balloon through the piece of tape. You will find that the balloon will not pop as the tape keeps the air in.

You may want to find the longest type of pin you can, but make sure it's not too thick.

Feeling adventurous? Try sticking the pin into the nipple of the balloon without the tape. The trick works this way too and is even more amazing. I like to have a volunteer inspect and inflate the balloon, that way they know it is not gimmicked.

Message: We have temptations everyday. Problems and people bring new challenges that we need to face in a manner that pleases God.

How can we do this? Through our faith in God. He has given us many promises that he will be with us through times of testing.

Ephesians 6:10-11,16 *Finally, my brethren, be strong in the Lord, and in the power of his might. Put on the whole armour of God, that ye may be able to stand against the wiles of the devil. Above all, taking the shield of faith, wherewith ye shall be able to quench all the **fiery darts** of the wicked.*

James 4:7 *Submit yourselves therefore to God. Resist the devil, and he will flee from you.*

1 John 4:4 *Ye are of God, little children, and have overcome them: because greater is he that is in you, than he that is in the world.*

The darts of the devil are like this pin to the balloon. But as the balloon is able to withstand, we also can stand strong on the Lord.

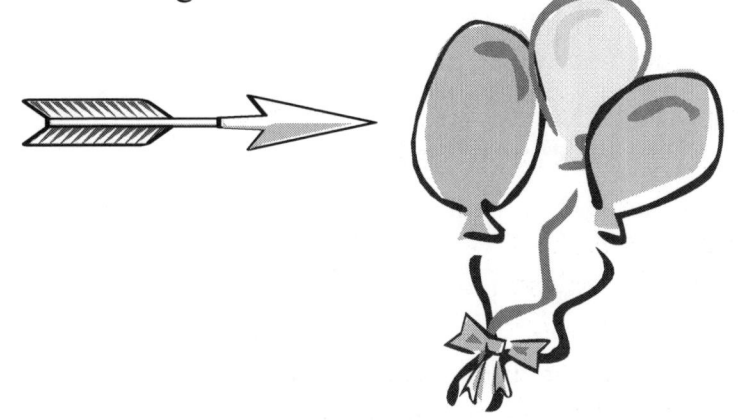

Week 23

"Spinning Pencil"

John 3:5-8 *Jesus answered, Verily, verily, I say unto thee, Except a man be born of water and [of] the Spirit, he cannot enter into the kingdom of God. That which is born of the flesh is flesh; and that which is born of the Spirit is spirit. Marvel not that I said unto thee, Ye must be born again. The wind bloweth where it listeth, and thou hearest the sound thereof, but canst not tell whence it cometh, and whither it goeth: so is every one that is born of the Spirit.*

Take a standard wooden pencil, preferably with flat edges (doesn't have a rounded body), place it on the edge of a table and balance it so it freely spins at the lightest touch.

Do this quickly so the audience doesn't suspect anything. Then wave your fingers around the pencil in a circular motion like you are summoning the power to move it.

Then lightly blow on it while the audience is focused on the pencil. It will seemingly follow your fingertips without you having ever touched it! It takes practice to get your breath to hit it without moving your mouth much, you want to be as subtle as possible!

Message: As the pencil is moved by an invisible power, so the power of the Holy Spirit moves within us to direct us.

Week 24

Spinning Egg

John 15:5 *I am the vine, ye are the branches: He that abideth in me, and I in him, the same bringeth forth much fruit: for without me ye can do nothing.*

Spinning egg effect: You spin an egg on the table and it spins well. When the spectator tries, he couldn't make the egg spin very well at all.

Secret: the egg you use is hard boiled and the egg the spectator uses is raw.

Presentation: You show a dish of five eggs and you should know which egg is the hard boiled one.

Instruct the spectator to point to one. If he points to the hard boiled one, tell him you will get that and he picks a different one for him.

If he points to the raw one, tell him he is going to use that one and you choose one (making sure you remember to pick up the hard boiled one).

Now spin your egg and ask the spectator if he could do it.

Message: We can struggle through this life, trying to do things under our own power. The results at best will be shaky, like when the volunteer spins his egg. Through the power of Christ in us, we can do all things, to his glory.

Week 25

Lazarus Arise

John 11:43 *And when he thus had spoken, he cried with a loud voice, Lazarus, come forth.*

Effect: This trick involves taking a matchbox and taping a piece of thin fishing wire on the bottom inside of it. Tie a paper clip to the other side and clip it on your pants. Place the string so it goes under your arm and through your fingers. Play around with it and you can get the matchbox to move, stand up by itself and even open.

Message: Tell the story of Lazarus. There was no life in Lazarus' body. Yet when Jesus spoke, it came to life. The matchbox seemed to come to life when I spoke to it.

> Like Lazarus, we need to hear the words of life, God's Holy Bible. It will manifest God's power in our lives as we read, hear, believe and act upon it.

Week 26

Quick Vanishing Match

Proverbs 23:5 *Wilt thou set thine eyes upon that which is not? for riches certainly make themselves wings; they fly away as an eagle toward heaven.*

Effect: A match is held in one hand right before the spectator's eyes. With a sudden jolt of your hand, the match disappears.

Secret : The non-striking end of the match is moistened with saliva and placed between forefinger and thumb. As you open your hand (rapidly) the forefinger releases it's hold on the match and the match remains "stuck" to the back of your thumb (Not visible to spectator). The Thumb is hidden behind your open hand.

You may now show the spectator your completely empty hands (While the match is concealed behind your thumb!!

Message: The things of this world are temporary. They can be gone in a flash. Rather we ought to lay up treasures in Heaven. These treasures are the rewards for doing right and last for ever. Paul discusses several crowns in the New Testament that the believer can look forward to in Heaven.

Week 27

Math Square Numbers

Job 21:22 *Shall [any] teach God knowledge? seeing he judgeth those that are high.*

Effect: Rapidly square a random two digit number.

Method: This magical math trick involves square numbers. Remember, you get a square number by multiplying a number by itself. For example 6 x 6 = 36. 36 is a square number.

There is an amazingly quick way of squaring a two digit number which ends in 5. All you have to do is multiply the first digit by the number one more than it, and then put a 25 on the end of your answer.

Example: 35 squared
3 x 4 = 12
put 25 on the end makes 1225

Note: this only works for two digit numbers that end in 5.

Presentation: Give a volunteer a calculator. Have another volunteer give you any two digit number ending with 5. You instantly give the answer and the calculator verifies your accuracy.

Message: God's knowledge is far superior than ours. Just as you demonstrate your superior math skills, so God shows his great knowledge everyday.

It is important that we read our Bibles daily to learn what the Lord would have us know.

Man's knowledge can be flawed, but God's is perfect.

Week 28

In A Twinkle Of An Eye

1 Thessalonians 4:17 *Then we which are alive [and] remain shall be caught up together with them in the clouds, to meet the Lord in the air: and so shall we ever be with the Lord.*

Effect: Make a card vanish into thin air!

Needed:
- Ordinary deck of cards
- Handkerchief with a hem
- Toothpick
- Scissors

Preparation: Take a toothpick and match it up against the end of one of the cards. Take the scissors and cut the toothpick so it's the same as the width of the card. Poke it into the hem of the handkerchief. Make sure it won't fall out.

Performance: Take the deck of cards and spread them out in a pile on the table in front of the audience.

Bring out your handkerchief and say, "I will make an ordinary playing card disappear, right before your very eyes," or something similar.

Place the handkerchief on top of the pile of cards, with the part with the toothpick underneath the rest of the handkerchief. Look casual as you do this.

With one hand, pick up the toothpick between your thumb and forefinger and raise it up from the pile of cards. It will look like you are holding the edge of one of the cards.

Say, "And it's gone!" as you wave the handkerchief in the air, showing there's no card inside. It's vanished into thin air!

Message: The Lord has promised to return for his church. As part of the body of believers, we need to be looking for his return.

Our preparation includes repenting of sin, making restitution where we can and being witnesses for the Lord. We need to share the gospel with everyone we can as the Lord's return draws nigh.

Week 29

Confetti Egg (Be Not Deceived)

Romans 7:11 *For sin, taking occasion by the commandment, deceived me, and by it slew me.*

Effect: An egg is placed under a handkerchief and is crushed The performer makes a disgusted face which suddenly turns to a smile as he unwraps the mess which has changed to confetti.

Method: Take a raw egg and make two pin holes in opposite ends lightly blow in one of the holes until the yolk pushes itself out the other side. Then fill the egg with confetti and seal the holes with some glue or putty. You can place the egg in someone else's fridge if you want add your own performance to this.

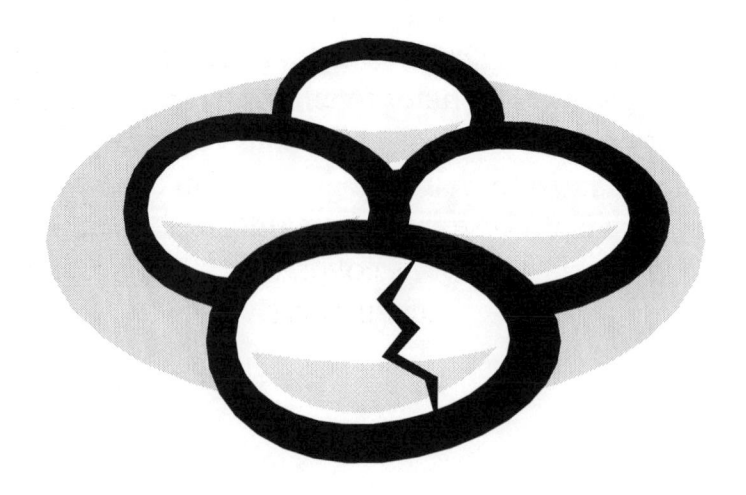

Message: God warns us many times in the Bible not to be deceived.

We should not be deceived by keeping bad company.
1 Corinthians 15:33 *Be not deceived: evil communications corrupt good manners.*

We should not be deceived by false religion.
Deuteronomy 11:16 *Take heed to yourselves, that your heart be not deceived, and ye turn aside, and serve other gods, and worship them;*

We should not be deceived by things of this world by trusting in our looks, health or wealth.
Job 15:31 *Let not him that is deceived trust in vanity: for vanity shall be his recompence.*

We should not be deceived by false teachers. We must study God's word so we will know the truth.
Luke 21:8 *And he said, Take heed that ye be not deceived: for many shall come in my name, saying, I am [Christ]; and the time draweth near: go ye not therefore after them.*

You could also use this trick to illustrate that we can not judge a book by its cover. It is what is inside us that matters.

Week 30
Disappearing Hanky

2 Corinthians 5:17 *Therefore if any man be in Christ, he is a new creature: old things are passed away; behold, all things are become new.*

Effect: You slowly stuff a handkerchief into your hand. With a magical wave of the other hand, you open two empty hands to the delight of the audience.

Method: To do this fabulous effect, you need to get a plastic egg, and some elastic. With the plastic egg, you cut a hole in it, so that you can stuff the handkerchief into it.

At the bottom of the egg, you run an elastic out, so that you can attach it to the inside back of your coat, and once you let go of the egg, it will fly to the inside back of your coat.

Now, when it looks like you are stuffing the handkerchief into your hand, you're actually putting it into the egg. Once there, while everyone is looking at your other hand, you let go of the egg.

Message: When we are born again, we are made a new creature in Christ. He takes away our sins (as represented by the hankey) never to remember them against us again.

Week 31

Handkerchief Knot

Isaiah 59:1 *Behold, the LORD'S hand is not shortened, that it cannot save; neither his ear heavy, that it cannot hear.*

Method: Pull a handkerchief out of your pocket, keeping the knot hidden in your hand.

Pick up the opposite corner of the handkerchief with the opposite hand, and grasp it.

Snap the handkerchief, releasing the end without the knot. Pick up the hanging end with the other hand as before and repeat, again releasing the end without the knot.

On the third try, let go of the knotted end, instead of the expected corner. The movement of the hand conceals the switch, and makes this a very baffling effect.

Presentation: Explain how you can tie a knot with one hand. Then demonstrate.

   Message: God needs only one hand to deliver us. Even in time of trouble, we can trust the Lord.

Week 32

Salt Shaker Through The Table

Hebrews 8:13 *In that he saith, A new covenant, he hath made the first old. Now that which decayeth and waxeth old is ready to vanish away.*

Needed: : Salt shaker and two paper napkins or one cloth napkin

Method: Cover the salt shaker with the napkins.

Next you form the cloth onto the salt shaker.

Then you pull the salt shaker towards you.

You distract your audience and drop the salt shaker into your lap.

Next you set the napkin on the table. It should hold its shape and look like the shaker is still under it.

Quickly bring your palm down on the napkin, flattening it against the table. It will appear the shaker has vanished.

Next you pull the salt shaker out from underneath the table.

Message: God promised the old covenant including the Law of Moses would pass away and he replaced it with the covenant of grace. Christ's death and resurrection fulfilled the demands of the law. We can now enter the kingdom of God through faith in Christ.

Week 33
Appearing Wand

Jonah 4:6,7 *And the LORD God prepared a gourd, and made it to come up over Jonah, that it might be a shadow over his head, to deliver him from his grief. So Jonah was exceeding glad of the gourd. But God prepared a worm when the morning rose the next day, and it smote the gourd that it withered.*

Effect: From a small purse you produce a large solid stick.

Method: Obtain a small money purse and cut a small hole at the bottom. Make a wand from a long piece of dowel.

Presentation: Have the wand partly up your sleeve and the other end inside the purse, through the hole. Show the purse, then open it and slowly pull out the large wand. This impressive illusion should be practiced in front of a mirror.

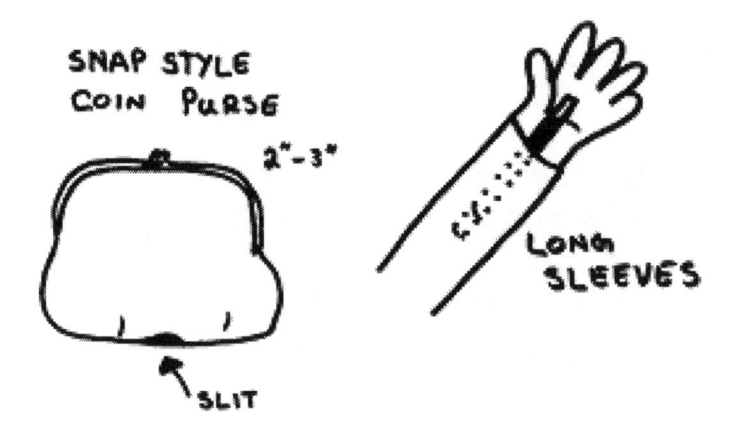

Message: The wand grows quickly like the gourd over Jonah. God provided Jonah shade and comfort in his grief.

GOD IS IN OUR COMFORTS: "God prepared a gourd." Everything of good that we enjoy, however little it may be, comes from God.

Now we turn to our second point, where we shall need even more faith than in the first part of our subject. The prophet next says that "God prepared a worm," which teaches us that GOD IS IN OUR BEREAVEMENTS AND LOSSES.

God also wants to provide for our needs and comfort us in times of trouble and sorrow.

The author, Dennis Regling, preaching at Camp Victory, KY

Week 34

Card To Matchbox

Exodus 7:10 *And Moses and Aaron went in unto Pharaoh, and they did so as the LORD had commanded: and Aaron cast down his rod before Pharaoh, and before his servants, and it became a serpent.*

Effect: A playing card changes into a matchbox

Method: Trim a playing card and glue it to the top of a matchbox. Carefully fold the card over the box. Glue a matchbox label on the back of the card so when the card is folded it looks like an ordinary matchbox.

Presentation: Show your audience the playing card. The matchbox is hidden behind it. Bring your hand over the card and secretly fold it up over the box. Remove your hand and it seems that you have made a playing card change magically into a matchbox.

Message: I like to discuss how God worked miracles through Moses, but Pharaoh's magicians could only imitate God's power, not duplicate it.

Real power in this life comes from God not from man.

Week 35
Stand Up For Jesus

Ephesians 6:13 *Wherefore take unto you the whole armour of God, that ye may be able to withstand in the evil day, and having done all, to stand.*

Effect: Make a handkerchief move up and down at your command as if it is standing up.

Needed: Handkerchief with a hem, drinking straw

Preparation: Carefully flatten a drinking straw. Next sew the straw into the hem of a handkerchief. Make sure the straw can't move within the hem as show in Figure 1. If your handkerchief does not have a seam, sew one in two of the sides.

Performance: When you are ready to perform the trick, take the corner marked with an "A" in Figure 1 and tie a knot in that corner. Hold the handkerchief with your right hand from the corner with the knot and let it hang down.

Figure 1.

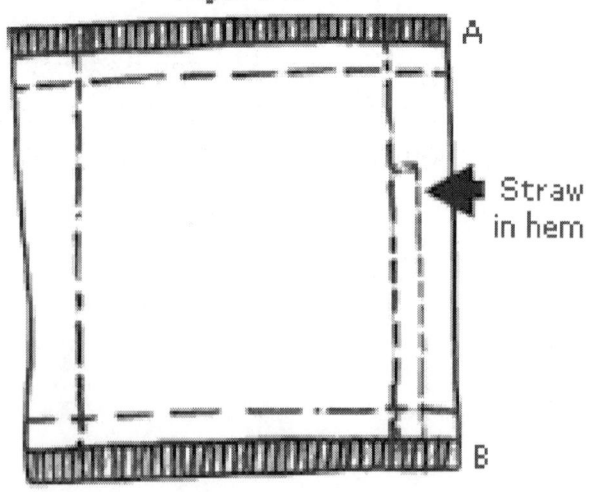

Tell the straw to "stand up for Jesus." With your left hand take the middle of the handkerchief where corner "B" is, as shown in Figure 2, and let go of the handkerchief with your right hand.

By slowly squeezing the straw with your thumb, you can cause the handkerchief to slowly rise as if it is standing up as shown in Figure 3.

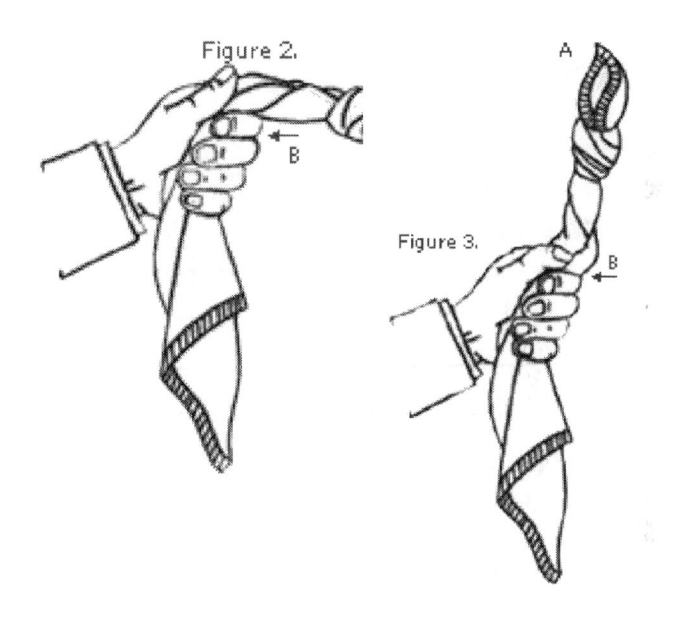

Figure 2.

Figure 3.

Message: We need to decide what we believe and take a stand. We need to stand for Jesus in our behavior, in our appearance and in our words.

Week 36

Escaping Match - Peter Escapes.

Acts 12:6-9 *And when Herod would have brought him forth, the same night Peter was sleeping between two soldiers, bound with two chains: and the keepers before the door kept the prison. And, behold, the angel of the Lord came upon [him], and a light shined in the prison: and he smote Peter on the side, and raised him up, saying, Arise up quickly. And his chains fell off from [his] hands. And the angel said unto him, Gird thyself, and bind on thy sandals. And so he did. And he saith unto him, Cast thy garment about thee, and follow me. And he went out, and followed him; and wist not that it was true which was done by the angel; but thought he saw a vision.*

Preparation: Before you start slide a match between the cover of a full matchbox and the bottom of the tray. Make sure this match faces the same way as the matches in the box.

In front of the audience open the box and remove the cover with your right hand. keep hold of the tray and the match underneath it with your left hand.

Carefully replace the cover holding the end of the match with your left thumb. Make sure the match stays outside the cover. Holding the end of the match with your left thumb make sure the match stays outside the cover and hold it there with your thumb.

Hold the box over a friend's hand and give it a tap let the match drop into her or he's hand it looks as if it has escaped through the bottom of the match box.

Message: The Lord delivers us in the time of trials. He will never forsake us.

Hebrews 3:5 *Let your] conversation [be] without covetousness; [and be] content with such things as ye have: for he hath said, I will never leave thee, nor forsake thee.*

Week 37

Mental Cups

John 3:8 *The wind bloweth where it listeth, and thou hearest the sound thereof, but canst not tell whence it cometh, and whither it goeth: so is every one that is born of the Spirit.*

Effect: magician moves a paper cup without touching it.

Preparation : Get some invisible string or a fishing line and wrap the ends of the string around your fingers.

Method: Have a spectator place a paper cup on top of the table. Put your hands around the cup and move it with the "invisible string" that is in the middle of your hand. Pretend that you are blowing the cup. When the spectator thinks that they have found out the secret to the trick, repeat the process and prove them wrong.

Message: In God's kingdom, there is a spiritual Helper who produces new life.

His role is to bring about "second birth" (John 3:5-8).

The Holy Spirit uses a variety of ways to accomplish this. He convicts the world of sin (John 16:8), empowers the gospel (1 Thess. 1:5), regenerates us from within (Titus 3:5), and places believers into eternal union with Christ (1 Cor. 12:12-13).

Though He is invisible, His life-changing activity can be clearly seen.

Jesus said of the Holy Spirit: *"The wind bloweth where it listeth, and thou hearest the sound thereof, but canst not tell whence it cometh, and whither it goeth: so is every one that is born of the Spirit."*
John 3:8

Week 38

Bills From Nowhere

Matthew 17:27 *Notwithstanding, lest we should offend them, go thou to the sea, and cast an hook, and take up the fish that first cometh up; and when thou hast opened his mouth, thou shalt find a piece of money: that take, and give unto them for me and thee.*

You must wear a blazer or a long sleeve, baggy top.

Preparation: Take a stack of five or six one-dollar bills. Roll them tightly. Place the bills in the fold on the top of the elbow of the left arm. Pull the fabric of the sleeve over the money and keep the arm slightly bent in order to keep them in place.

Performance: With the bills in position face the spectator. Pull up your left sleeve from your elbow to show you have nothing on your wrist. During this move grasp the bills from the crook of your sleeve with right hand and conceal them in your palm. Do the same with the right arm to show you have nothing there, either. Now put both hands together and reveal the magic in whatever way you think best.

Message: God provides for his people.

Week 39
Pins Thru The Thumb

John 20:25 *The other disciples therefore said unto him, We have seen the Lord. But he said unto them, Except I shall see in his hands the print of the nails, and put my finger into the print of the nails, and thrust my hand into his side, I will not believe.*

Effect: Magician inserts pins through a cloth into his thumb. A story of faith.

Preparations: Place a carrot in a cloth napkin

Method: You place the cloth napkin over your hand, stating you will drive a number of pins through his thumb. The magician has a small carrot hidden in the napkin. When you place the napkin over your hand, you put your thumb down and place the carrot up through your fist, so as to resemble the thumb. Then you stick pins through the cloth and into the carrot. After driving all the pins through the carrot, carefully remove each pin, drop the carrot back into the napkin while removing it, and reveal your thumb to the crowd.

Tips: While driving the pins in, you should have a look of pain and make it appear as though the pins are hard to get in, and are hurting you.

Message: Thomas did not believe Christ had risen, even though Jesus had said he would. We need to trust God's word even when it makes no sense to us in the natural.

God's word is true and his promises will always be kept.

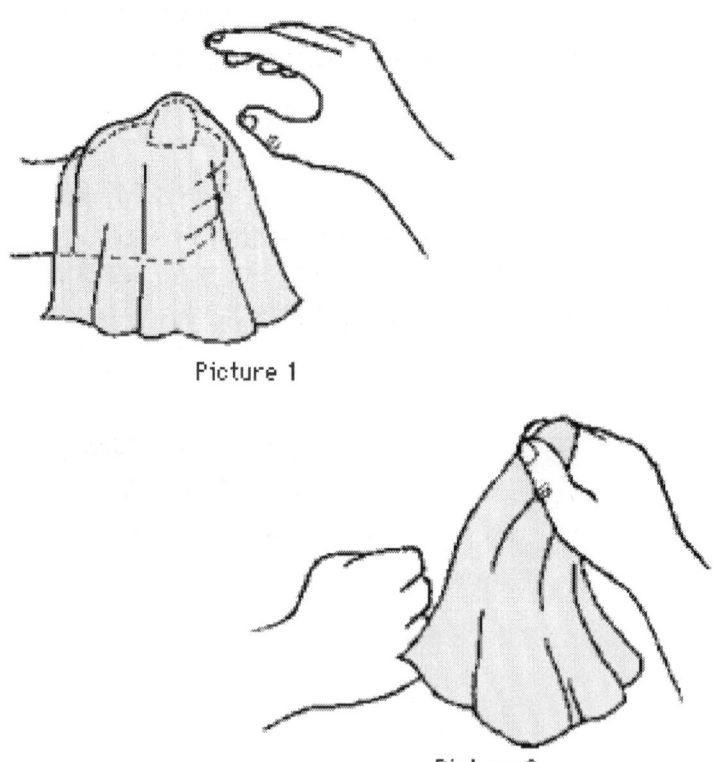

Picture 1

Picture 2

Week 40

Ropes Thru The Body

2 Peter 2:20 *For if after they have escaped the pollutions of the world through the knowledge of the Lord and Saviour Jesus Christ, they are again entangled therein, and overcome, the latter end is worse with them than the beginning.*

EFFECT: Take 2 lengths of rope around your back. You tie the top rope in a tight half knot around your body. Now 2 members of the audience pull the ropes totally through the magicians body!

METHOD: All the you need to do is tuck the 2 ropes separately down the back of your trousers. Then continue the trick as described above. As long as the ropes are separate and do not get in a tangle, the trick will work perfectly.

Message: We are not to get entangled with sin and bad activities. If we do, Jesus is ready to forgive us and set us free, when we turn to him.

Week 41

A Ticket To Heaven

John 14:6 *Jesus saith unto him, I am the way, the truth, and the life: no man cometh unto the Father, but by me.*

Needed: an 8.5" x 11" sheet of paper, a scissors.

Fold the top left corner to the right side of the paper, forming a triangle, then the point at the top right over to the left side of the paper. Now it looks like a house with a pitched roof. Now fold the paper in half and hold it at the folded side.

Presentation: There was a man who saw another man with a ticket to heaven, and the man demanded a portion of his ticket. (At the open end of the paper, cut a piece off, bottom to top, and hand it to the demanding man.) So the man gave him a piece of his ticket. The demanding man decided that if he had just a little more of the ticket, he would receive more rewards in Heaven. (At the open end, bottom to top, cut off another piece and give it to him.) The demanding man with the pieces of the ticket went before God and presented it to him. God said, "This ticket shows me that you are not my son."
 (Use the cut pieces to spell out 'Hell'.)

Then, the man who gave the pieces away, presented his ticket to God. (Unfold the large paper to reveal the cross.) God said to him, "This shows that you are my son. Welcome to Heaven!"

Jesus said, "*I am the way, the truth, and the life: no man cometh unto the Father, but by me.*" **John 14:6**

Jesus suffered and sacrificed himself on the cross for our sins. He offers us the only way to heaven. Do you have your ticket?

Message: We cannot get to heaven on our own merits, or anyone else's for that matter. Being born into a Christian home, knowing the right people, or behaving a certain way, doesn't get you to heaven.

Only Jesus has the power to cleanse us of our sins and make us presentable to God.

Ephesians 2:8-10 *For by grace are ye saved through faith; and that not of yourselves: [it is] the gift of God: Not of works, lest any man should boast. For we are his workmanship, created in Christ Jesus unto good works, which God hath before ordained that we should walk in them.*

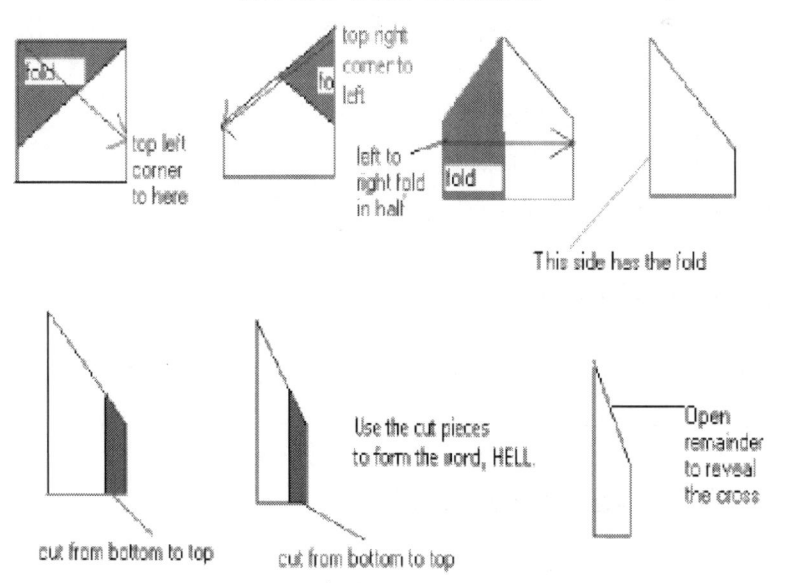

top left corner to here

top right corner to left

left to right fold in half

fold

This side has the fold

cut from bottom to top

cut from bottom to top

Use the cut pieces to form the word, HELL.

Open remainder to reveal the cross

Week 42

Indestructible Laces (God's Indestructible Word)

Matthew 24:35 *Heaven and earth shall pass away, but my words shall not pass away.*

Effect : A lace is fed thru the straw, the straw is cut in half, the laces are still in one piece

Preparation:
Take a straw and make a slit through the length of the straw stopping about 2' from each end. Now tell the audience that these laces are indestructible and bend the straw in half. Make sure the slit is at the bottom and pull on the lace it should come through the slit leaving no lace in the middle of the straw. Now cut the straw where there is no lace. After you have cut the straw use your hand to cover the cut then pull out the lace and wait for the applause.

Message: God's Word, the Bible stands forever. Man rewrites his books on evolution, philosophy and science every few years, but God's word never changes.

Week 43
Swiss Movement

Ephesians 6:13 *Wherefore take unto you the whole armour of God, that ye may be able to withstand in the evil day, and having done all, to stand.*

Effect: You need a Swiss army knife and a credit card. After some hullaballo you try to balance the knife on it, but fail. Then, you remember something, and pull the blades out in various poses. When you balance it, it stands perfectly and can even move side to side.

Materials: A credit card, and a Swiss army knife (make sure it has the little tweezers)

Method: Tell your audience that you are going to perform a difficult feat, requiring both natural balance, and mental power.

Hold up the credit card directly vertical, and try to place the closed knife on it pointing straight up. Make sure to drop it, giving the impression that this is hard to accomplish.

Place the knife on the card, concentrating very hard. Pull out the little tweezers and hold with thumb.
It will look like knife is balancing on the credit card. At this point make it look like this is taking great deal of effort.

Put up your other hand and wave it near the knife. At the same time move your other thumb to look like your hand is controlling movement of the knife.
After this is done for a little while push tweezers back in. You can hand everything back for examination.

Week 44

Word Prediction

Luke 8:17 *For nothing is secret, that shall not be made manifest; neither any thing hid, that shall not be known and come abroad.*

Effect: Give someone a paperback book. Ask them to hold the book behind their back and open to a page. (Even they can't see their page selection.)

Hand them a thin marker and tell them to draw an "X" on one of the pages. Telling them to close the book and to hold it between their hands. You will then take a pen and write the word on a piece of paper. Now tell the person to look for the x. Your prediction and the marked word match!
Ask your volunteer to open the book and find the marked page. One word has the "X" through it. You open your prediction - they match!

Method: First you need a paperback book, a piece of paper, and two thin marking pens. You need to prepare for this, so take the book and find a page near the center of the book with words covering the entire page. Take the pen and mark a big "X" across the page. Don't be neat, this has to look like he drew it behind his back. Notice the word that the x intersects with. Memorize it. Then you have to prepare one of the marking pens. Take it and dry it out so it no longer works or coat it with wax. Make sure it cannot mark. This is the marker your volunteer uses.

Week 45
The Two Ball Effect

Acts 8:39 *And when they were come up out of the water, the Spirit of the Lord caught away Philip, that the eunuch saw him no more: and he went on his way rejoicing.*

The effect: You make a small ball vanish from your hand and appear in a volunteer's hand.

Needed: A volunteer and two small balls made out of soft material. Sponge Balls are best. (You can tear a paper napkin into two pieces. Each piece can be rolled into a satisfactory ball.)

Method: With your right hand pick up one of the balls. Hold it so that your fingers touch and your thumb holds the ball in place. If you hold your hand palm down, the ball will be hidden from your audience's view. This is called "palming". Pretend to put the ball into your left hand. Don't make a point of this. Close your left fingers "around it". You merely "rake" the ball across the open palm of your left hand as you close it around empty air. In reality, you keep the ball in your right hand. This is called the "rake-through vanish". Practice in front of a mirror until you can't see the difference between actually leaving the ball in your left hand and secretly taking it away with your right hand. Put the ball that is concealed in your right hand on top of the ball on the table. Pick them both up as one. Put them both into your volunteer's hand. Ask him to squeeze tightly. Then have him blow on your left hand. Slowly open your left hand and show that the ball has vanished. Have him open his hand and notice his amazement when he sees both balls.

Week 46
The Filling of The Holy Spirit

1 John 4:4 *Ye are of God, little children, and have overcome them: because greater is he that is in you, than he that is in the world.*

Effect: Water is poured into an empty cup. When it is turned over, the water remains.

Needed: A foam cup, a glass of water, slush powder

Method: Put a tablespoon of slush powder in the bottom of the foam cup. You can show the cup to be empty, since the white powder will be hidden against the white color of the cup. When water is poured into the cup, it forms a gel that will stay in the cup when it is inverted.

Message: When we believe on the Lord Jesus Christ, he sends his Holy Spirit to dwell within us. This cup represents our life. Before we are saved, our life is empty of God. (Show empty cup.)

I will pour water into the cup, showing how God pours his Spirit into us. Even when the world turns us upside down with troubles, God does not leave us. (Turn cup upside down. Water remains in cup.)

Jesus gives us his Holy Spirit to comfort us and to give us power to be his witnesses.

Matthew 28:19-20 *Go ye therefore, and teach all nations, baptizing them in the name of the Father, and of the Son, and of the Holy Ghost: Teaching them to observe all things whatsoever I have commanded you: and, lo, I am with you alway, even unto the end of the world. Amen.*

John 14:27 *Peace I leave with you, my peace I give unto you: not as the world giveth, give I unto you. Let not your heart be troubled, neither let it be afraid.*

DIAPER CHEMISTRY

Ask the mother of a baby for a disposable diaper. Make sure it is a clean diaper.

Cut open the diaper and hold it over a newspaper. A powder will fall out of the diaper. This powder is called Sodium Polyacrylate. Magicians call it slush powder.

It is perfectly safe, but be sure not to get it in your eyes.

Sodium Polyacrylate powder is a super absorbent. I call it a chemical sponge.

When water is added to the white crystalline powder, it absorbs the water like a sponge. As it absorbs the water, the tiny pieces get bigger and form a gel.

Disposable diapers use small amounts of Sodium Polyacrylate to absorb baby urine.

The more polymer powder in a diaper, the more urine it can absorb.

Week 47

Rising Dough

1 Corinthians 15:51 *Behold, I shew you a mystery; We shall not all sleep, but we shall all be changed,*

Effect: A dinner roll is placed on a plate and is covered with a handkerchief. Grab two ends of the handkerchief and the dinner roll mysteriously rises up with the handkerchief, then back down.

Needed: Plate, Dinner Roll, Fork, Handkerchief/Scarf

Settings: Must be done at a table, sitting in a chair

Method: Under cover of the scarf, stab the fork into the roll. Hold the fork handle between thumb and forefinger at the corner of the scarf. Hold the other corner in your other hand. You can now lift the scarf and manipulate the roll behind the napkin.

Have it push forward on the napkin or peek over the top. Practice until you can make it look almost alive.

It helps to nonchalantly prepare the roll and fork before you start the trick.

Message: One day we will meet Jesus in the sky. Our bodies will be changed from corruptible to incorruptible. Are we ready to meet the Lord?

Week 48

Card Switch

2 Corinthians 5:17 *Therefore if any man be in Christ, he is a new creature: old things are passed away; behold, all things are become new.*

Effect: Show the Jack of Diamonds on top of a deck of cards. Place it in the spectator's hand. Have him place the other hand on top. Now show the top card as the Jack of Clubs. The cards then change places.

Method: The only sleight is the double lift. To perform the double lift, square the deck and lift the top two cards as one. You must have two Jack of Clubs. Have the Jack of Clubs on top of the deck, Jack of Diamonds on top of that and the next Jack of Clubs on top of that.

Presentation: Double lift to show the Jack of Diamonds, place back on top of deck and remove top card (Jack of Clubs) and sandwich in the spectators hands. Double lift to again show the 2nd Jack of Clubs and place back on deck remove top card (Jack of Diamonds) and wave it face down over the spectators hands, turn it over to reveal the Jack of Diamonds whilst the spectator looks at his/her card to find the Jack of Clubs.

Message: When we are born again, we are changed. Old desires will be replaced with new desires as we study the Bible and walk with Christ.

Week 49

Falling Quarter - Wealth is Fleeting

Matthew 6:19, 20: *Lay not up for yourselves treasures upon earth, where moth and rust doth corrupt, and where thieves break through and steal: But lay up for yourselves treasures in heaven, where neither moth nor rust doth corrupt, and where thieves do not break through nor steal:*

1) Take a quarter or other coin in your right hand.

2) Turn to a member of the audience and ask them to stand. Hold the coin in your thumb and index finger, and say if when you count to three they can grab the coin, they can keep it.

3) Raise the coin above your head and bring it down to the volunteer's open hand twice, counting each time aloud. On the third time lift the coin above your head and place it gently and subtly on top of your head.

4) Bring your hand down as you did before to the level of your volunteer's open hand.

They will make a swipe at the coin, but it will have vanished. Open both hands to show them it's truly gone. Then tell them you'll bring back the coin. Hold their hand open and while their attention is directed to their own hand, tilt your head forward ever so slightly. The coin will drop into their hand, seemingly out of the sky.

Week 50

The Dissolving Coin

2 Kings 6:5-7 *But as one was felling a beam, the axe head fell into the water: and he cried, and said, Alas, master! for it was borrowed. And the man of God said, Where fell it? And he shewed him the place. And he cut down a stick, and cast [it] in thither; and the iron did swim. Therefore said he, Take [it] up to thee. And he put out his hand, and took it.*

The Effect: A coin is taken in a handkerchief. The handkerchief is placed over a glass of water and the coin is dropped in. The audience sees the coin in the glass, then upon a second look, the coin has dissolved out of the glass.

Presentation: In order to do this effect, you need a clear glass cup, with no special bottom. Hold the glass in one hand, and put the handkerchief over your other with the coin on top of the handkerchief. Slide the coin between your index finger and thumb, and cover the water filled glass the first time.

Tilt it by raising your fingers upwards. This is unknown to the audience.

After that, the coin is held in the handkerchief, above the tilted outside of the glass. When it is dropped, it should strike the outside of the glass then it slides into your fingers. The noise makes the audience think the coin landed inside the glass, but you just maneuver it under the glass so that it really looks like it is in the glass.

Allow the audience to look straight down at the coin when showing it to them.

Then, cover the glass back up with the handkerchief, and grab the top of the glass. You put the glass down on the table with the handkerchief over it. Secretly, the coin will be in your opposite hand, which you nonchalantly slide into your pocket, drop the coin, and slide it back out while you're removing the handkerchief from the glass.

Message: The axe head, lost in the water is rescued. God cares about the everyday things.

Philippians 4:6 *Be careful for nothing; but in every thing by prayer and supplication with thanksgiving let your requests be made known unto God.*

Week 51

Cut-N-Restored Rope

The cut and restored rope has literally hundreds of variations. Practice it well and it will prove to be quite effective.

Effect: A 5 foot rope is displayed and examined. Hold both ends together to locate the center of the rope. The rope is cut in two and the cut ends tied together. Then the knot is removed from the rope which is again in one piece.

Method: After the rope is examined, hold both ends in your left hand. Reach through the hanging loop with your right index finger just left of the center of the rope at point C (Figure 1). With your thumb and middle finger on the outside of the loop, lift the center as if to place it in your left hand.
As your right hand approaches your left hand, reach through the loop with your right thumb and middle finger and grab point D, a few inches below end B and pull it through loop C (Fig 2).

Bring loop D up into your left hand, hiding the real center of the rope in the palm of your left hand (Figure 3).

The audience thinks they see both ends and the middle of the rope above your left fist.

Cut loop D and hold both ends of the small piece that you cut off, letting the other ends fall (Fig 4).

Tie a knot in the short piece at its location in the middle of the long piece and it will look like two halves of the rope tied together.

To restore the rope just slide the knot off one end or you can wrap the rope around your left hand, sliding the knot off with your right as you go. Experiment with it and come up with your own ideas!

Application: For Gospel applications I mention that we often have problems in our lives that are difficult to face. Sometimes the problems are the result of our own doing, and sometimes there's nothing we can do to avoid them. If we rely on our own resources, the best we can do often leaves "knotty" problems that continue to get in our way. But when we let God take over he can take us through.

Sometimes He completely removes the problem, and sometimes He uses the problem to strengthen us, but He is always there to restore and renew us.

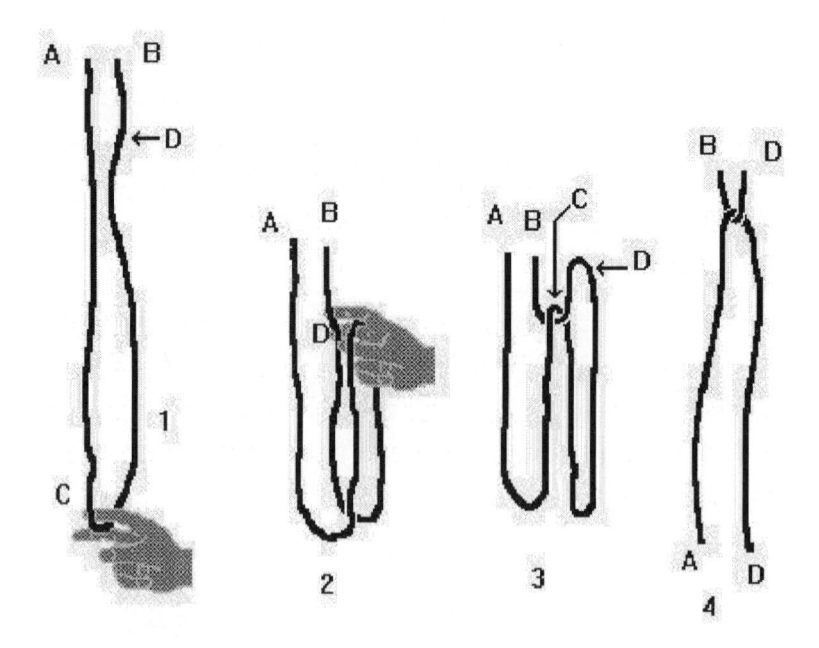

Week 52

Be Set Free

John 8:36 *"If the Son therefore shall make you free, ye shall be free indeed."*

Effect: Two volunteers are selected from the audience. The ends of a rope are tied around each wrist of one volunteer. The same is done with the second, but before tying, the ropes are linked together.

The volunteers are challenged to separate without removing the ropes.

Needed: Two soft ropes, 3-4 feet long.

Application: The Bible teaches that all of us are sinners. It just comes natural for us to do the wrong thing. Even when we really want to do what is right, we eventually do something wrong.

We can try all kinds of self-help programs or 12-step plans, but ultimately, our problem lies in our own inner nature. In **Romans 7** the apostle Paul talked about his struggle with his sinful nature, and asked the agonizing question *"Who shall deliver me from this body of death?"*

Thankfully, Paul goes on to chapter 8 where he finds the answer in Jesus Christ. Only He can set us free from our sins and empower us to live a holy life. As we daily yield to Jesus, He can set us free from the sins that drag us down.

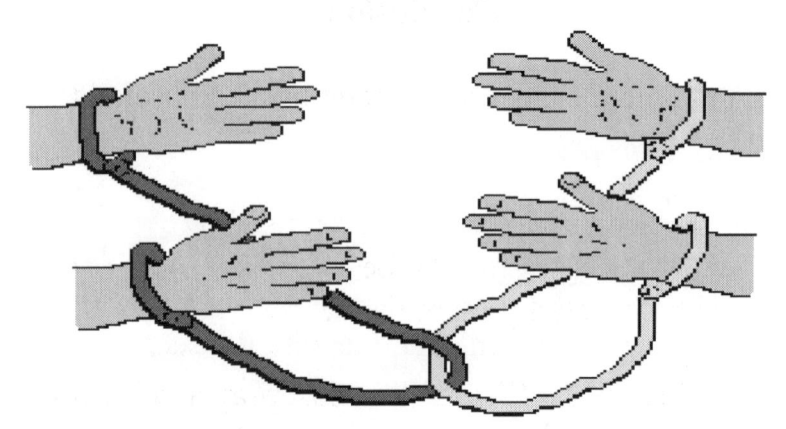

Method: To separate the two volunteers, take the middle of one rope up through the loop around the other person's wrist. The rope should be on the front side of the wrist. Pull enough rope through the loop to go over the hand and then pull it out on the back side of the hand. If done according to the pictures above, the two volunteers will now be free of each other.

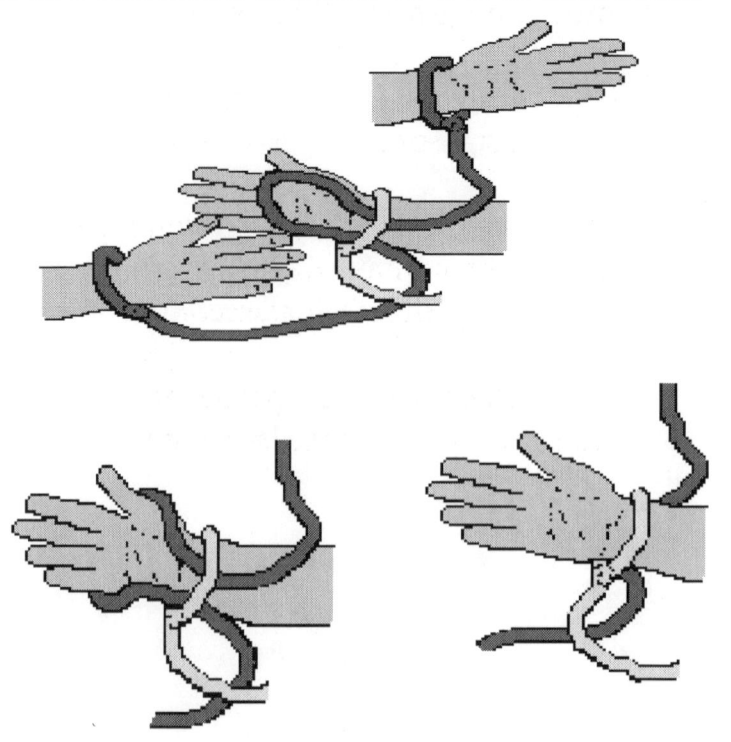

Conclusion

You have here 52 object lessons using household items.

These are good tricks and are even used by professional magicians. To be effective, you must practice before you present them.

To be effective for Christ, you must pray and let him empower you for his service. You need to look up the Bible verses and read the verses in context. Then, you must use the effects to relate the message God has put on your heart.

It's not the tricks that will change lives, it is the Gospel and Bible truths presented with the power of the Holy Spirit through a sanctified vessel.

The ideas in this book can be used for devotional purposes or as the start of a longer sermon.

God bless you as you serve him. If you have any questions, do not hesitate to email Dennis at::
Dennis@BibleDefender.com

To purchase some Gospel Magic:
http://www.magicministry.com

ABOUT THE AUTHOR

"Mr. Dennis" Regling lives in Freeport, Ohio with his wife Karen and several cats. Freeport is a small town nestled in the foothills of the Appalachian Mountains.

Dennis and Karen are members of Ebenezer Baptist Church. They are active in youth ministry and prison ministry.

Dennis presents programs at Vacation Bible Schools, Sunday Schools, children's fairs, Bible Camps, and Christian schools. Dennis is also available for fair ministry, public outreach programs and soul-winning.

Dennis has performed educational programs in over 1200 schools in 22 states.

Dennis and Karen are available for programs for your group. Dennis can be contacted at (740) 658-4336

Alpena Baptist Church

Pastor Benjamin Brown

Dear Brothers in Christ,

I am writing this to recommend my friend and co-laborer, Evangelist Dennis Regling. He is a willing servant of God. He is a preacher of the Bible, handling the Word of God with caution and skill to bring forth a message from God to speak to the hearts of the people. I believe he will be a blessing to you and your people. May God richly bless you, as you seek to do His will!

In Christ,

Benjamin A. Brown
Micah 6:8

Pastor Benjamin A. Brown
Pastor of the Alpena Baptist Church

350 Pinecrest St. Alpena, MI 49707 (989) 354-8557

Notes:

Made in the USA
San Bernardino, CA
08 December 2012